AF605418

JOHN LESLEY

GREEN SEA TURTLE

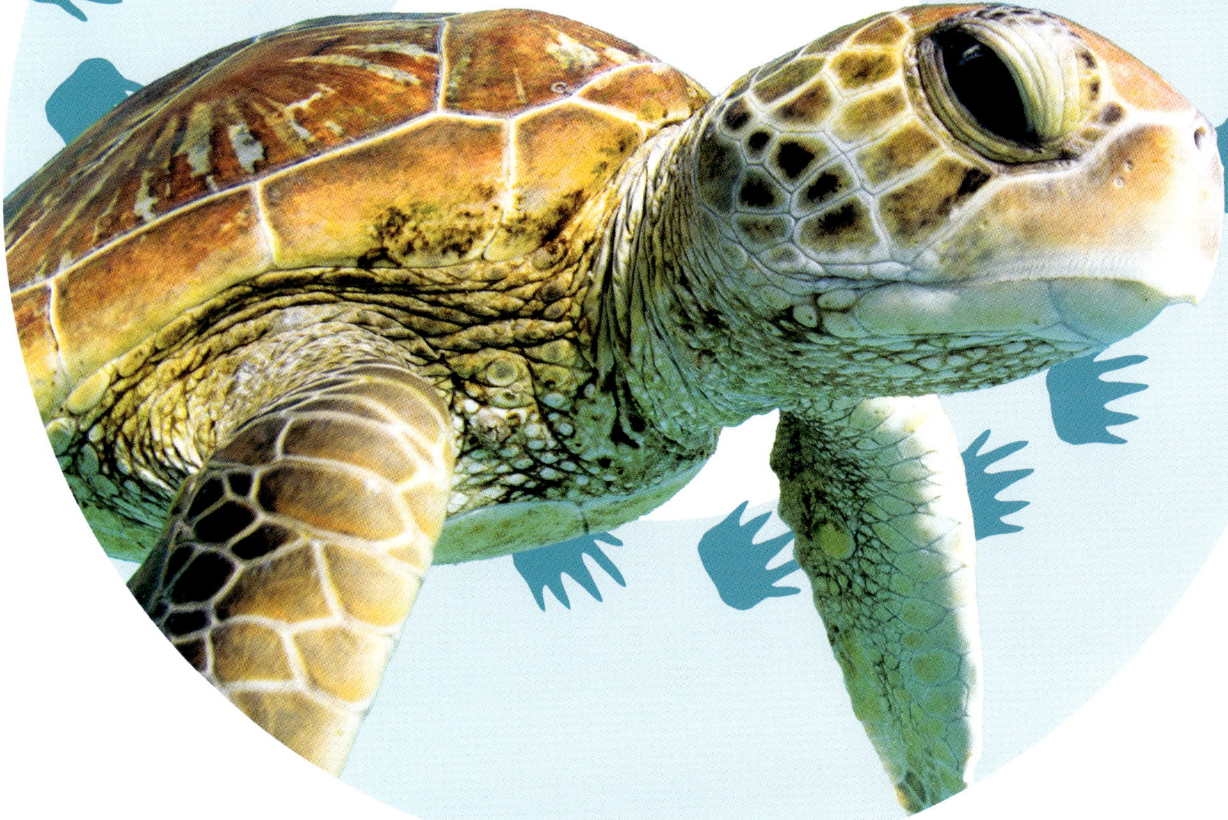

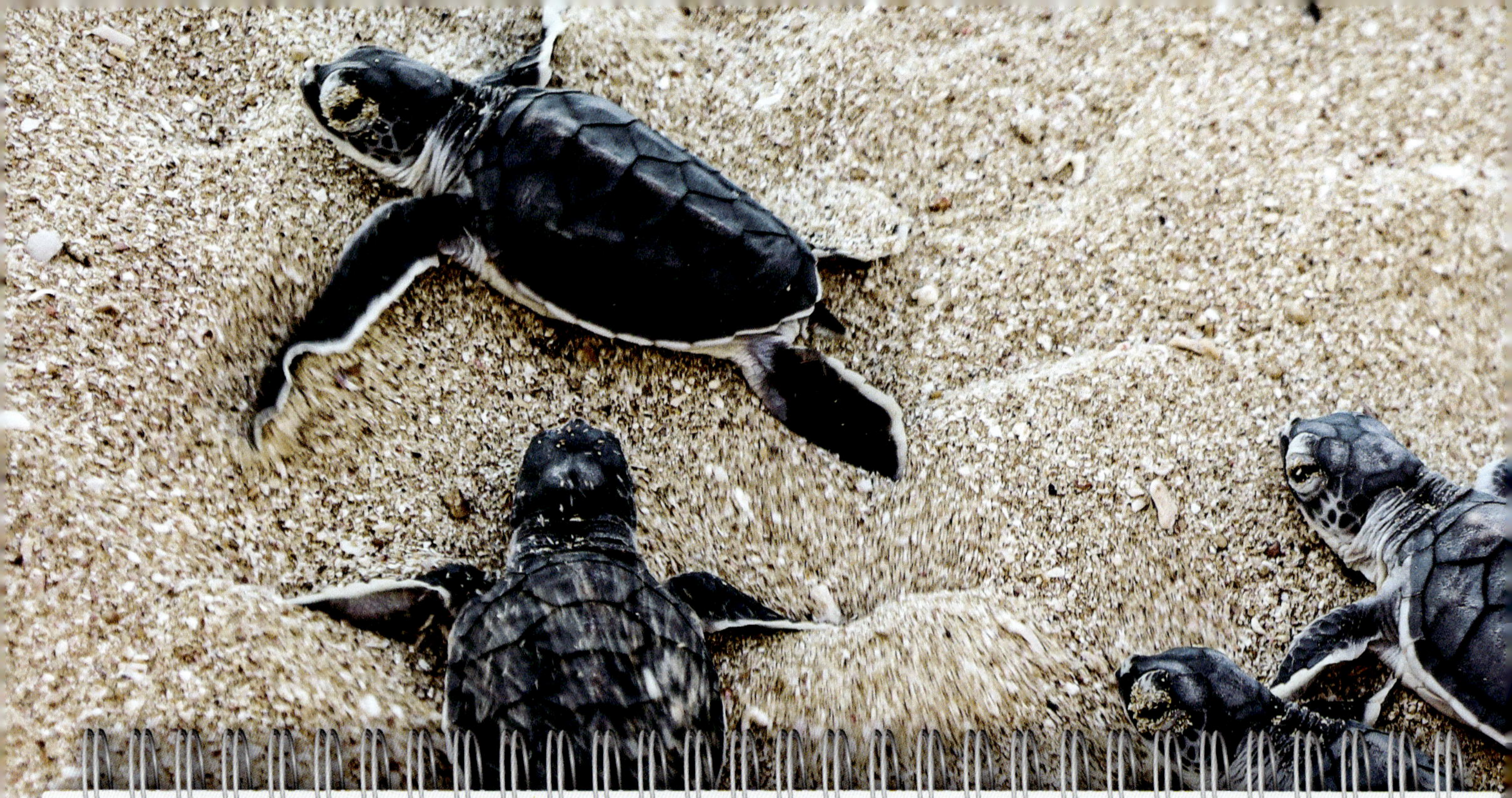

First Published 2025
Redback Publishing
Suite 6, 13a Narabang Way,
Belrose NSW 2085
Australia

www.redbackpublishing.com
orders@redbackpublishing.com

ISBN 978-1-761401-34-3

Author: John Lesley
Editors: Lucinda Dodds and Emma Dobinson
Design: Redback Publishing

A catalogue record for this book is available from the National Library of Australia

Originated by Redback Publishing

Acknowledgements
Abbreviations: l—left, r—right, b—bottom, t—top, c—centre, m—middle
We would like to thank the following for permission to reproduce photographs: (Images © shutterstock)

CONTENTS

WHAT IS A GREEN SEA TURTLE?

Green sea turtles are animal citizens of the world. They live in warm ocean waters and lay their eggs on beaches in many countries.

Despite their international range, local populations have developed and one of these is the green sea turtle population that regularly visits the Great Barrier Reef. There is also another group that is found further south along the Australian coast.

Each of these populations around the world are the same species, but geography keeps the groups separate. For example, a green sea turtle of the Pacific Ocean is likely to stay there throughout its life, rather than trying to find a way to enter the Atlantic Ocean, which would mean swimming through cold, southern waters.

All turtles are reptiles. The turtle shell is made of bone. It is attached to the backbone and ribs.

EAST AUSTRALIAN CURRENT

The East Australian Current wasn't well-known before it was portrayed in the movie *Finding Nemo*. In this movie, a green sea turtle uses this strong ocean current to take a leisurely ride from place to place in the Pacific Ocean.

GREEN SEA TURTLE BASIC FACTS

SCIENTIFIC NAME

Chelonia mydas

REPTILE

The green sea turtle is an aquatic reptile. It lives its whole life in the sea, except for when the female lays her eggs on a beach. The young race into the water as quickly as they can after hatching.

CRYING

Green sea turtles on land often look as though they are crying. The water running from their eyes is very salty and is an adaptation that allows the turtle to remove some of the salt that it has consumed in the ocean.

They are big!
Wildlife workers who rescue stranded green sea turtles need special sleds and trolleys to carry them because they are so heavy.

GREEN SEA TURTLE BODY

GREEN?

The term 'green' does not describe the outer colour of the green sea turtle. It actually refers to the green fat inside the turtle, which comes from its diet of green plants.

SHELL AND FLIPPERS

The shell and flippers can be black, brown or a mixture of these colours. The underside of the shell and inside of the flippers are often a cream colour. In shallow water above a seagrass meadow, the light can sometimes make a brown turtle look green or blue. Hatchlings have a cream line around the edges of their shell and flippers.

WEIGHT:
Grow to over 200 kilograms

SHELL LENGTH:
Grow to 1.5 metres long

FACT:
The green sea turtle cannot pull its whole head into its shell for protection

HEAD AND BEAK

The mouth has a beak on the top jaw and rough edges on the lower jaw, which enable the turtle to feed on plants by tearing off mouthfuls.

BREATHING UNDER WATER

Green sea turtles are aquatic, but they have lungs like land animals. Although they spend most of their time under the water, they still need to come up for air, taking one big breath that can last for hours. If they are feeding or moving quickly, they need to breathe more often, but when they are sleeping their use of oxygen slows down remarkably.

Watch a turtle closely when it comes up for air, and you will see it gulp in a big breath.

If trapped in a fishing net in the ocean, a turtle will drown.

Green sea turtles have developed special adaptations that allow them to hold their breath for a very long time. They can reduce their heart rate when they are in the sea, and their blood can hold a higher amount of oxygen than land animals.

GREEN SEA TURTLE MIGRATION

Green sea turtles are migrators. They swim thousands of kilometres away from where they are born, looking for food.

Decades later, when they are mature, they usually return to the same beach where they hatched out of an egg. They find a mate, leave their eggs behind, and start their migration all over again.

They find their way across the planet using the Sun, smell and also the Earth's magnetic fields. Traces of magnetic iron in their bodies may allow them to sense the magnetic lines that cross the planet, and then follow them to find their way around.

The green sea turtles of the Great Barrier Reef migrate to the islands north of Australia before returning to the reef to breed. They only make this massive migration every few years, as they do not breed each year.

How far a green sea turtles migrates is different for each turtle, but the reason for this is not yet known.

Many parts of the migration journey of turtles are still a mystery to scientists.

GREEN SEA TURTLE HABITAT

All turtles are reptiles, so they need a warm environment. Green sea turtles live in warm tropical and subtropical water. In Australia, the Great Barrier Reef has a large breeding population that returns there annually. Some turtles also swim as far south as the southern coast of Australia.

The habitat that a green sea turtle needs changes as it ages. The hatchlings leave the beach and stay in shallow water. The juveniles move further out along the continental shelf under the sea. The adults swim in the open ocean but stay close to the land. Most of the green sea turtle nesting sites in Australia are in Queensland.

Juveniles need access to small sea creatures to eat, so they stay in shallow reefs.

GREEN SEA TURTLE LIFECYCLE

EGGS

Like other reptiles, green sea turtle babies hatch out of eggs. In Australia, these are laid during the spring and summer.

Male turtles hatch from eggs that are kept cool, but female turtles hatch when the eggs get hot. Climate change might have a disastrous effect on the future numbers of green sea turtles if too many females are born. Breeding requires both males and females, so too many of the one sex will result in fewer hatchlings being born.

Green sea turtle eggs look like ping pong balls.

If it survives, a baby green sea turtle can live for 90 years.

After mating, the female turtle drags her heavy body up onto a beach, which is very likely to be the same one where she hatched as a baby 40 years before. She digs a hole with her back flippers and lays up to 100 eggs about half a metre deep in the sand. The eggs are soft, white and round.

HATCHLINGS

After covering the nest well, the female makes her way back to the ocean. The hatchlings come out a few weeks later, at night. They fight their way out of the sand and try to get to the water before they are eaten by predators. Juveniles take about 30 years to become old enough to breed and lay eggs.

WHAT THEY EAT

Green sea turtles change what they eat as they age.

The hatchlings are omnivores. They eat what they can find, including worms, shrimp, grass, plants, small fish and fish eggs. As they age, they become herbivores. At this stage, they need lush underwater meadows of seagrass to feed on, although they also eat other underwater plants.

Green sea turtles have an important role in keeping the seagrass healthy. As they feed on it, they take only the tips, encouraging the seagrass to grow thickly. This is a benefit to all the other ocean life that also needs seagrass to survive.

PLASTIC

Turtles browsing on plants can mistake green plastic for food. Once inside them, the plastic can block their digestive system causing them to starve to death.

Adult green sea turtles only eat plants, but other big turtles can mistake a plastic bag for a jellyfish and try to eat it.

PREDATORS OF GREEN SEA TURTLES

A 200 kilogram green sea turtle has few predators on land or in the ocean. Large sharks, whales and humans are a few of the creatures that can kill an adult turtle. An older turtle can swim fast considering its weight and shape, so it can escape from some predators in the ocean.

When the turtles are young, predators are everywhere. Only a very small percentage of hatchlings survive to become adults. Predators know when it is time for hatchlings to emerge from the nest under the sand, and they wait.

Hatchling and a dingo

Eagles, seagulls, foxes, dingoes, feral dogs, sharks, crocodiles and crabs all feast on the babies.

A turtle's shell can become infested with barnacles that slow it down when swimming. Sea leeches attach themselves to turtle skin and may weaken the turtle through blood loss.

GREEN SEA TURTLES AND PEOPLE

ENDANGERED

Catching or harming a green sea turtle is a serious offence in Australia and in many other countries. They are endangered and threatened with extinction across the world, due to ocean pollution, poaching and loss of seagrass meadows due to changes made by humans to the environment.

PLASTIC AND POLLUTION

Plastic pollution starves turtles by becoming stuck in their bodies after they eat it because it looks like food. Pollution of seagrass meadows and other parts of the ocean badly affects turtles at every stage of their lifecycle.

BITES

Green sea turtles have strong, hard mouths. They can bite if provoked, producing a serious wound. They are mostly very easy going and rarely bite in anger. Keeping your distance from a wild animal is always a good idea, no matter what the animal is or where you are.

Turtles browsing on seagrass are often severely injured by boat propellers.

FISHING NETS

Although green sea turtles are aquatic, they need to come to the surface regularly to take a deep breath. Being caught in a fishing net and held under the water will cause a green sea turtle to drown.

THE HUMAN IMPACT

In the past, green sea turtles were killed for their shells and to make leather out of their skin. Turtle soup, made from green sea turtles, was once served in the best restaurants around the world. Commercial killing is now illegal in Australia.

All around the Pacific Ocean, indigenous people have been catching turtles and using them for food and for cultural purposes for many thousands of years.

TURTLE NESTING SITES

RAINE ISLAND

Raine Island in the Great Barrier Reef is the largest green sea turtle nesting site in Australia, and also one of the biggest in the world. The island is formed from a buildup of coral over thousands of years. It is a protected zone and visiting is not allowed.

The island's boundaries change from time to time due to natural causes. This has resulted in turtle nests being flooded by the ocean. To help the endangered green sea turtles survive, parts of the island have been reshaped to make them safer for nesting.

Satellite transmitter on a green sea turtle

Scientists have attached satellite trackers to green sea turtles so they can find out how far they travel across the ocean.

Here are just a few of the sites in Australia where green sea turtles come ashore:

MARINE TURTLES IN AUSTRALIA

There are a number of other species of marine turtles, besides the green sea turtle, that visit Australian oceans:

FLATBACK TURTLE

Natator depressus

The flatback turtle only breeds in Australia. It lives in the sea near Indonesia, Papua New Guinea and Australia's north and northeast coast. Flatback turtles prefer shallow, soft-bottomed seabed habitats away from reefs, and they feed on jellyfish, sea cucumbers and soft corals.

OLIVE RIDLEY TURTLE

Lepidochelys olivacea

Many hundreds of female olive ridley turtles can leave the sea to lay their eggs at the same time on the same beach. This is probably an adaptation that protects the babies when they hatch, leading to more being able to reach the sea before being taken by predators.

Flatback turtle

Olive ridley turtle

LEATHERBACK TURTLE

Dermochelys coriacea

The leatherback turtle can grow to a huge size and is the largest turtle in the world. The shell is covered in leathery skin, which gives this turtle its name. They can grow to over two metres long and weigh up to an amazing 500 kilograms!

HAWKSBILL TURTLE

Eretmochelys imbricata

The hawksbill turtle feeds on sponges and algae, using the sharp tip of its beak to break off pieces that are easy for it to swallow. They look similar to the green sea turtle, but the pointed beak is a way to tell them apart.

LOGGERHEAD TURTLE

Caretta caretta

The loggerhead turtle's shell has a more elongated shape than that of the green sea turtle. They feed mostly on crabs, shellfish, sea urchins and jellyfish.

TURTLE OR TORTOISE?

What is the difference between a turtle and a tortoise?

Green sea turtle

TURTLE	TORTOISE
Webbed feet or flippers	Feet with claws
Aquatic, living most of their life in water	Live on land, but may spend some time in water
Flatter shell for swimming through water	Dome shaped shell
Many turtles visit the ocean around Australia, and some freshwater species live in rivers and lakes	Australia does not have any native tortoises

Giant Galapagos tortoise

A true tortoise lives only on land. A famous example is the giant Galapagos tortoise.

There are many species of freshwater turtles in Australia. Here are just a few:

Some people use the term 'tortoise' for Australia's native freshwater turtles. This helps to separate them from the marine turtles in the sea around the coast.

SORTING ANIMALS INTO GROUPS

Biologists divide all living things around the world into groups. They call this process classification. The two basic groups of animals are called:

Vertebrates are further divided into five groups called classes. Humans are in the class called Mammalia. **Green sea turtles are reptiles and belong in the class called Reptilia.**

INVERTEBRATES
Invertebrates do not have a backbone

VERTEBRATES
Vertebrates have a backbone

AMPHIBIANS
(Amphibia)

MAMMALS
(Mammalia)

REPTILES
(Reptilia)

BIRDS
(Aves)

FISH

GLOSSARY

aquatic living in water

barnacle small sea creature that attaches itself to rocks, turtles or whales and then builds a shell around itself

herbivore animal that eats only plants

infested having a lot of parasites or unwanted creatures in or on the body or in a place

juvenile baby that has started to grow up

lungs body organ that allows animals to breathe air

ocean current flow of water like a river within the ocean

omnivore animal that eats both meat and plants

oxygen gas in the air needed by animals to live

vertebrate animal with a backbone

INDEX